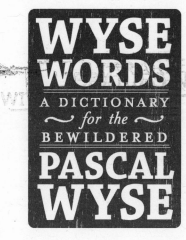

WYSE WORDS

A DICTIONARY
~ for the ~
BEWILDERED

PASCAL WYSE

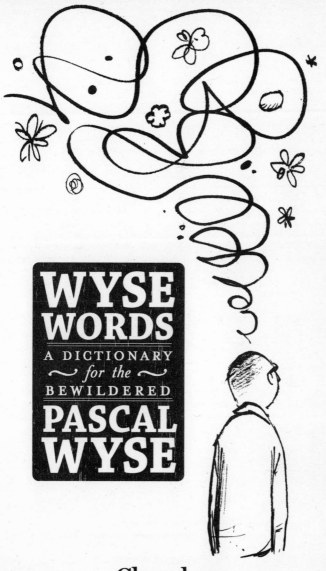

WYSE WORDS

A DICTIONARY
~ *for the* ~
BEWILDERED

PASCAL WYSE

Chambers

CHAMBERS
An imprint of Chambers Harrap Publishers Ltd
7 Hopetoun Crescent, Edinburgh, EH7 4AY

Chambers Harrap is an Hachette UK company

Text © Pascal Wyse 2009
Images © Joe Berger 2009

Chambers® is a registered trademark of Chambers Harrap Publishers Ltd

First published by Chambers Harrap Publishers Ltd 2009

A CIP catalogue record for this book is available from the British Library.

ISBN 978 0550 10474 8

10 9 8 7 6 5 4 3 2 1

We have made every effort to mark as such all words which we believe to be trademarks. We should also like to make it clear that the presence of a word in the dictionary, whether marked or unmarked, in no way affects its legal status as a trademark.

www.chambersharrap.co.uk

Designed by Chambers Harrap Publishers Ltd, Edinburgh
Typeset in Didot by raspberryhmac graphic design
Illustrations by Iain McIntosh
Printed and bound in Great Britain by

For mum and dad

Acknowledgements

Many thanks to Merope, who first commissioned some of these words for the *Guardian Weekend* magazine, and to Liese, who then edited them (ie saved me from myself and sent them back when they weren't good enough). Thanks to Morven, my editor at Chambers, for her undying enthusiasm and patience faced with my initial reluctance to write a book (ie do some work); to the copy editor Graeme for his excellent suggestions; to Joe for his trusty judgement and great illustrations; and to Camilla for all her advice and steering. Name-checking family, friends and readers who have offered ideas for entries would run the risk of me missing someone out, but thanks to all of you. Finally, thanks to Helen.

Introduction

I have a fond memory of a Christmas day some time in the 1980s, when my dad, finally relieved of present distribution duties (we like to make a protracted deal of it in our family, one gift at a time), disappeared into an armchair with a book he and mum had bought me: *The Meaning of Liff*, by Douglas Adams and John Lloyd. It was a dictionary that took village, town and city names from the UK and gave them definitions relating to everyday life.

After a period of studious silence, my dad began chuckling. Not guffawing, just burbling away contentedly. It was a particular kind of laugh that sticks in my memory. Once I got my hands on the book, I realised – or, to be more honest, I can now conveniently post-rationalise – that it had something to do with relief and recognition. It was someone else picking up on an aspect of life that you had noticed, or that niggled you, but perhaps you had assumed was just part of your peculiar outlook. It was a reassuring answer to the call: "There should be a word for that." (I can't boil an egg without thinking of how, in Liff, the pleasing little spoonful you dig out of the lid once you have chopped it off is called Symonds Yat.)

Enough larding someone else's book with praise. As Dr Johnson, the godfather of the dictionary, said: "Almost all absurdity of conduct arises from the imitation of those whom we cannot resemble." But times have moved on, and there are new things to catalogue, quantify and quiz over. It doesn't take much detective work to deduce that, looking at the title of this publication, I'm the one who is bewildered. So this dictionary is my attempt, my distress signal, to locate others who have noticed these foibles, and who may get some comfort or amusement from the fact that they have been written down. Then perhaps we can all join up and form a super-race of confused people, leave Earth to colonise a new world and be really bewildered together and shout in to our mobile phones: "I'm on another planet!"

On the other hand, it may all just prove that I have a peculiar outlook on life. In which case, this dictionary, I hope, will give readers a warm reminder of just how well-balanced and tolerant they are.

WYSE
WORDS

abbababba

noun

The language of the wedding DJ. To sober people it amounts to little more than the sound of a moped being revved up. To drunk ears it is a hunting call: "The dancefloor is your kingdom. You are its ruler. You are made of sex."

addiversary

noun

Annoying tendency of actors to harmonise any rendition of *Happy Birthday*.

aglumni

noun

A peculiar kind of melancholy brought on by looking at your old CVs.

agrobat

noun

Someone who, by repeatedly insisting you are annoyed, makes you annoyed, even though you weren't.

alcatholicism

noun

The guilty assumption that since you can't remember what you did at the end of an evening's drinking it must have been quite awful.

ancest

noun

The socially paralysing effect of sex appearing on TV while you are watching with your parents..

apocollapse

noun

A moment of blood-fizzing rage powerful enough to make you talk to inanimate objects such as hammers. Yes, they are involved in a global conspiracy to pervert the course of your DIY, but tools are trained to resist blunt interrogation tactics such as "Why can't you just do what I want?".

apolojeer

noun

The art of saying sorry in a totally superior way. The trick is to sound wracked with genuine concern but subliminally convey a withering disdain for how pathetic the other person is for taking whatever you said to heart. Then get them to say sorry for getting you to say sorry.

◆ **apolojeerer**

noun

Bb

baghetti
noun
The seedy, somewhat apprehensive feeling a man gets when rifling through his girlfriend's handbag – even when he has been given permission to do so.

bagpluss
noun
The reassuring feeling of weight on your legs when you go to bed without removing the CLOAD that you placed on it that morning when you got up.

bapaslapa
plural noun
The unique hand movements used by chefs to

fashion a pizza base out of a ball of dough. Like fighting with a wet hat.

beercut
noun
An injury whose cause cannot be remembered the following day.

beerwigs
noun
The mysterious pile of flotsam you often find on pub tables. This totemic gathering of peeled beermats, tiny foil figures and obsessively compacted peanut packets is like a memorial to a previous drinker.

belottle
verb
To begrudgingly admit that someone is really great.
◆ **belottler**
noun

beltranté
noun
1. A mildly aggravated tone of voice used by people who think things should be done for them because they are very beautiful.

bewble

2. A person who does things for others purely because they are very beautiful.

bewble
noun
The thing you buy for yourself when you should be shopping for a gift.

bidgits
noun
An inability to take your eyes off a progress bar on a computer screen, even though the whole point of a progress bar is to let you know the computer will be a little time doing its thing, and you should get on with your life, except for the moment you seem to have misplaced your life.

billoiter
verb
To hang around slightly too long after paying in a restaurant in order to make sure the waiter sees that you have left a tip.
◖billoiterer
noun

bink
noun
The process of gingerly parking a car in a tight

spot by waiting for your bumper to hit the car
behind.
◢ **binker**
noun

biografear
noun
Insecure reluctance to admit you are not familiar
with a book or other cultural marker someone
you have just met feeds in to the conversation.
"Of course, I must have read it years ago — it
rings a familiar bell, but in a part of my brain I
haven't visited for some time." See also WITRAT.

biroid
noun
A person who feels the need to carry a significant
number of pens, either neatly arranged in a top
pocket or slotted carefully into a special briefcase
compartment.

blodger
noun
The most regular and committed poster of
comments on your blog, and the one that makes
the least sense.

blofft
noun

The special, chummy sound of an airline pilot's voice, designed to make everyone feel calm — a combination of poshness and just the right amount of boredom because flying is so easy a chimp could do it. After a few years practice, any distinct words disappear altogether, and all that remains is a smooth, reassuring burble.

blogorrhoea
verb

Endlessly reloading your own blog – like a rat who has been trained to press a button to get a fix of heroin – in the hope of seeing the comments count go up.

blubatorium
plural noun

The seconds of calm consideration a toddler takes after falling over. This gives time for the little team of crash investigators inside his head to rush to the scene and assess damage, parental liability and candy-extortion potential. A decision is then made as to whether it's worth crying.

blubbits

plural noun

Spots of adhesive on a wall that demarcate the ghosts of previous tenants and their posters.

blurbeyodle

noun

The dreamy, sing-song or zombie-like way of speaking that develops in anyone who has to say the same thing over and over again for their job, eg air stewards, train guards, dentists and roadies testing microphones. See also BLOFFT.

blutter

plural noun

Increasingly panicky attempts made by radio presenters to draw an interview to a close as the pips approach.

boap

noun

The sound of someone who insists on continuing to talk even though it is uncomfortably clear they need to stop and belch.

boke

plural noun

The forlorn, skeletal remains – left locked to a

bonoculars

railing – of a bicycle that has been plundered by
thieves for parts.

bonoculars
plural noun
Sunglasses needlessly worn indoors by posers
and rock stars.

boogle
noun
An unshakeable determination to locate a
book or CD yourself without the aid of a shop
assistant.

borchids
plural noun
The growth of empty beer bottles that
mysteriously appears in your garden on a
Saturday morning.

branky
noun
That amazing digestif you enjoyed after
each precious meal on your honeymoon in a
heavenly destination. You brought back four
litres, convinced that the mere whiff of it would
transport you once more to paradise. But in the
context of your own kitchen, it tastes foul.

brimpotence

noun
A stage in mid-life where, having not worn one for many years, thereby distancing oneself from the fashion follies of youth, you decide it is time to start wearing a hat again.

brittarded

plural noun
People who believe that foreigners will understand English if you just say it louder and slower.

broadshit

plural noun
The parts of a Sunday paper you immediately throw in the bin outside the newsagent.

broadwake

noun
The point in a celebrity's life where people can't quite remember whether they are dead or alive.

bronthesaurus

noun
Species of writer dedicated to using extinct modes of expression in order to give off a whiff of the classics.

blubatorium

broodcaster

noun

Someone who is able to bring any conversation, however esoteric or abstruse, round to the subject of their children.

◆ **broodcast**
verb

budgkinsons

noun

A paranoid belief that everyone at a crowded gig is making a conscious and malicious effort to choose a path through you to the toilets at the back.

bummerang

noun

The new way of walking you have to adopt if you like wearing your trousers in the hip-hop *Grand Old Duke of York* style: neither up nor down. To practise, half-undress and imagine passing a Space Hopper between your legs without letting your feet leave the ground.

buncle

noun

A friend or relative who insists on helping you with a DIY chore, arrives, completely takes over,

burytone

is rubbish at it, buggers the whole thing up, has a cup of tea, asks how your mum is, and leaves.

burytone
noun
Someone who sings with so much vibrato you have no idea what note they are actually trying to produce.

butternoths
noun
A condition of insecurity that causes people to express approximations of an idea instead of the real thing, usually prefaced with "I mean, not this, but …". A way of building in a get-out clause should the thought turn out to be embarrassingly bad.

Cc

calcaholics
plural noun
Scary folk who are able to tell you, down to the nearest minute, how much of your life you have spent doing mundane things such as brushing your teeth.

canappease
noun
Status-anxious smalltalk aimed at waiting staff at parties. Partly it just feels strange to relieve someone of salmon teriyaki without passing the time of day, but "Oooh, can I take two?" really means: "Look, I don't normally live like this. I am like you really. I'm a real human being."

chairvoyance

noun

An attempt at appearing casual about where
you are going to sit at a big table in a restaurant
when in fact you are furiously trying to predict
where the person who bores you to suicide is
going to sit and manoeuvre yourself to the other
end of the table.

chari-kiri

plural noun

Evasive actions needed when a charity mugger
has locked on to you — because you feel guilty
about not having one minute to help a child.
Normally involves pulling out your phone to
pretend a debilitatingly massive thought has just
occurred to you.

chatapap

noun

The staged cough, sniff or whistle you have to
do in order to prevent people barging in to a
lavatory that has no lock on the door. The real
art, requiring precise volume and timing, is to get
it to sound coincidental rather than panicked.
Some prefer the comfort of continuous
humming.

chavalanche

noun

A coachload of people brought in to whip up a frenzy of audience indignation on emotional porn shows such as Jerry Springer.

chellogs

noun

The scratchy four-minute message that is left, like a haunted dispatch, on your mobile at 3am by an unwittingly activated phone in someone's pocket.

◆ **chelloger**

noun

Person who unwittingly activates their phone in the middle of the night.

chidder

verb

To pretend to be annoyed with your child for the benefit of the parent of another child it has just upset, when in reality you think what just happened was hilarious and totally justified.

chipurine

noun

The smell of pubs.

choats

plural noun

The parts of their lives people leave behind on library desks, seats at the cricket or tables in bars to indicate that a seat is in use by them — even if they don't return for another three years.

choim

noun

Dispiriting breakfast assembled from the dust at the bottom of various cereal packets.

chronanism

noun

Watching a movie you already have the DVD of, just because it is on the telly; Googling ex lovers; contemplating a cheese diary; starting a charity bag; experimenting with screensavers … The special collection of vague activities that gets you from 11pm (when you were totally ready for bed) to 1.30am (when you actually retire).

chumnesia

noun

The point in a friendship beyond which it becomes too embarrassing and insulting to confess that you never quite caught (or have forgotten) the person's name — since by this time you have already had long conversations at parties, had lunch together or, in extreme cases, been married for 10 years.

◆ **chumnesiac**
noun

cinemany
noun
The realisation, roughly two thirds of the way through, that you have already seen a film you are currently engrossed in while also recalling that the ending is a real disappointment.

circusised
noun
Having your enjoyment of a pleasant summer day in the park brutally cut short by the arrival of a troupe of amateur jugglers and acrobats, rehearsing their jesters' skills a little too close for comfort. The pleasure they have taken from you can never be recovered.

claperazzi
plural noun
Odious people who sit right down at the front of a Proms concert, ostentatiously following their own copy of the score of a piece of music purely so they can be the first to clap when the

piece is finished, thereby ruining the precious
few seconds of silent contemplation that should
follow a performance.

clatteracts
plural noun
Bizarre bird-like noises made by a group of
women who can't let each other finish any
sentences – a form of BLUTTING.

cload
noun
A pile of wardrobe-shy garments that has to be
repeatedly removed from the end of the bed each
night so you can get in, then picked up off the
floor and placed back on the bed in the morning
so you can walk around.
verb
To repeatedly remove garments from the end of
the bed each night so you can get in, then pick
them up off the floor and place back on the bed
in the morning so you can walk around.
◆ **cloader**
noun
A person who cloads.

clockroach

noun

The colleague who is always at work before you and unconsciously checks the time when you get in.

cloffin

noun

1. A bag of clothes intended for the charity shop that has been in the boot of the car, or hallway of the house, for over a year.
2. The smell of those clothes when bought from the charity shop.
3. Someone who specialises in wearing eccentric clothes purchased from a charity shop.

cnqt

noun

The sound you make when you are trying to scratch an itch that is right in the centre of your head, between your nose and mouth.

comediocrity

noun

A class of person that turns the simplest exchange into a conversational bramble bush. "I'm fine," you say. "I know you're fine, but do you want a drink?" they reply. "Is this chair free?"

you ask. "No, my tiny invisible friend is sitting there," they say.

commutant
noun
Someone who derives secret and immense pleasure from watching another traveller miss a train or bus they already have a seat on. Optimum satisfaction is gained from the flailing passenger who pretends, having slammed their whole body against a closing door, that they didn't really want to get that train after all.

complifications
plural noun
Well-intentioned moves assumed to be helpful in a given situation, but which make things infinitely worse — such as guests tidying your house when you are out so you will never find anything ever again, children putting a mucky gerbil in the dishwasher, or toddlers eating money for safekeeping.

complimince
noun
The art of sounding enthusiastic about the labours of a friend when you really think what they have done is rubbish – but without

involving yourself in any real dishonesty eg "Hey, you've really done it with this one. It's definitely got your feel."

condominimum
noun
An apartment, usually described by the estate agent as 'charmingly proportioned, sensitively modernised and ideally situated for local amenities' that turns out to be perfect if a flyover is an amenity, if 'sensitive' means 'not' and if you think it's cute that you can touch all the walls of your flat without getting out of bed.

condomint
noun
A prophylactic boasting a flavour you would barely consider eating if it belonged to a foodstuff, let alone a rubber sheath. Often obtainable from vending machines in the toilets of pubs that have been GASTRATED.

copscoff
noun
Branch of suspicious sarcasm used by police officers, bouncers and customs officials to talk to the general public. This sneer is actually a clever way of getting perfectly reasonable and innocent

circusised

people to explode with rage, necessitating arrest, a half-Nelson, and the treat of an elbow-deep cavity search.
♦ **copscoffing**
noun

cramplifier
noun
A tiny, cheap car with pointless, shiny racey-bits and a very loud sound system.

crampolene
noun
Special (often stupid) piece of clothing that only leaves the wardrobe for work Christmas parties. Despite straining in the crotch, and struggling with developments in your waistline, a quality CRAMPOLENE can last a lifetime, keeping you hip for roughly a tenth of your career. For the remainder you look like a pervert.

creabing
noun
The act of stealing someone else's cheese from the fridge, but in homeopathically small slices in the hope they won't notice. A culinary death by a thousand cuts.

crocodial

verb

To produce your mobile phone at a party and text urgently, or listen to an important message with a warm smile on your face, when in fact there is no message, and you are pretending to text — because no one is talking to you at this party. Your cellphone is your only friend.

◆ **crocodialler**

noun

One who participates in crocodialling,

croprastination

verb

To insistently get on with things that aren't ready to be done yet.

crustation

noun

A place to buy CRUSTICS.

crustics

plural noun

Restricted spectrum of mute, country colours that many gravitate towards for their clothing in old age, as if someone has turned down the contrast and colour controls of their life.

Dd

dadjectives
plural noun
Show-off words, often rather obscure or out of
character, that your father only uses when your
first girlfriend comes round to visit.

decravity
noun
That slightly saucy way some dentists report, in
code, the whereabouts of your teeth and lack of
teeth to their recently groped assistant.

deejade
noun
The point in your life when, despite having made
no conscious decision to stop, you seem to have
ceased going to nightclubs.

dialation

noun
Actor habit of staring into the handset after performing the dramatic and abrupt end to a telephone call.

dimbleby

noun
The haphazard walking style of someone who is going through severe episodes of GINSTINCT and ALCATHOLCISM, involving stopping, starting and sudden changes of direction in order to outrun the embarrassing images in their head.

dimsome

noun
Packaging that thinks you are too dense to work out what to do with the food inside, so offers handy hints such as 'Tear & Share', 'Stand 'N Stuff' and 'Eat'.

disastronauts

plural noun
People who float around curiously at the fringes of accidents and emergencies but don't get involved or help in any way.

discoast

noun

Jelly-limbed halfway point between walking and dancing that you go through when approaching (or leaving) a dancefloor. The transition has to be executed gradually, since suddenly rocking out looks a touch unhinged, while abruptly stopping your moves creates the impression you are going off in a huff because no one is paying attention.

discobobulate

noun

Casual, low energy dancing needed to pass the time while a DJ digs himself out of an especially challenging and clumsy mix between two tunes.

displeisure

noun

The tryanny of unfocused recreation — a day off work, or from wrangling the children, that feels so long-awaited and precious that when it arrives you end up paralysed with stress about the most fruitful way to use it. So you do nothing, or just go back to work in order to relax.

doctopus

noun

Someone who gets an irresistible urge to ask a

droogling

series of nagging medical questions of a doctor at a dinner party.

droogling
noun
Trying to find yourself on the internet when drunk.

drooring
plural noun
The final few nonsensical words you say while trying to maintain a conversation with a friend who is explaining their problems to you as you fall asleep on their sofa.

Ee

egonomics
noun
The process of revealing (as if it was of no consequence but clearly is) how much money you spent on the birthday present you just gave.

electrocity
noun
The shocking memory of George Bush.

emageddon
noun
The career apocalypse caused by a message — hypothetically, something like "I would rather hack off my head with a rancid chicken bone than work another day with Paul. He needs to be forced up his own ringpiece" — which in the

emphasimia

heat of the moment you accidentally send to
Paul, Paul being your boss.

emphasimia
noun
Exhaustion caused by reading texts with too
many exclamation marks!

emule
noun
The one gullible person in a million who
happily sends their bank details and password
in response to a global message from The Right
Rev Fulsome Horace Tabberspank, who claims to
need a safe place to secrete the $120 million he
was surprised to find had been left to him by a
deceased member of his congregation.
♦ **emuling**
noun

encrapsulate
verb
First, modestly rebuff the admiration of
someone who marvels at your understanding
of a complex subject. Then insist, appealing to
their intellectual vanity, that a person with their
brains could easily understand it as well. Finally,
make them feel like a fool by explaining it in

a deliberately complex and impenetrable way, thereby proving what they first thought: that you are marvellous.

enpsychopedias
plural noun
Infuriating books at a shop counter about wacky things such as *Why Prawns Can't File Their Own Income Tax*. Books such as the one you are holding.

enthusanasia
noun
The fake interest you have to summon when faced with things such as toddlers' games, other people's holiday snaps or being shown round a potential property you have already decided is completely horrible. Behind that fixed smile is the daydream of hundreds of estage agents' cars being driven off a cliff.

eraillment
noun
The way a series of short, fun emails goes suddenly quiet after one party actually bothers to sit down and write something thoughtful.

ergomaniac
noun
Someone whose house or flat is so designer it is impossible to tell if they actually have any possessions at all.
◆ **ergomania**
noun

excity
noun
A social gathering that involves various of your old partners meeting each other, and appearing to get on quite well, giving rise to a mild paranoia about what is being said about you.

Ff

fadvent
noun
The arrival of people camping outside a shop
to be the first to buy a NEWPID they are going to
want to replace within the year.

fagulation
noun
The attempt, as a non-smoker, to have a coherent
social experience with a group of smokers in a
pub who come and go in different combinations,
and occasionally leave you completely alone. Like
trying to conduct a meaningful conversation,
backstage during a show, with the cast of a
French farce.

flarebags

famex

noun

Someone who prepares for all the trappings of fame, such as deciding on the records they are going to play on *Desert Island Discs*, while forgetting to become famous.

fanaesthetist

noun

Someone who relishes telling you a devastating piece of gossip about a film star you are deeply in love with.

fanchovy

plural noun

Audience members who nod and say 'Yes', 'Exactly' and 'Mmmm' as if the person delivering a lecture to a packed theatre is talking to them, and only them.

fanticipation

noun

Distracting "Oh this bit coming up is brilliant" chat from a friend who decides to go and see a film with you that they have already seen and loved and are very keen that you like too, which you might if they would just shut up.

farmbands
noun
Rustic-looking packaging that very ordinary groceries are transferred to in order to give them a wholesome air of the organic and expensive.

fatomatics
noun
Branch of science used to predict the point at which a new year resolution will be abandoned. Knowing $h + r$ [hope plus resolve], and $s \times h$ [seductive value of habit multiplied by health threat] a result can be found to within an accuracy of $+/-$ two minutes, using self-hate as a constant.

fillywig
verb
To ruffle a child's hair as a kind of affectionate gesture – an action that has bewildered the young for hundreds of years.

finglish
plural noun
People who pepper their sentences with 'like' all the time.

fopulate

flaprosy
noun
Feeling compelled to wave at people just because
they are passing by on a boat. Even sociopathic
wrecks feel this urge for a fleeting episode of
shared humanity, though they counterbalance
it by secretly mumbling "I hope you go down,
losers" through a clenched smile.

flarebags
plural noun
Clothes that only look good when you are
jumping up, in mid-air, like models in fashion
shoots for heavy magazines that smell of
perfume.

flottered
noun
Confused state caused by wondering how to
interpret a compliment that is well beyond its
sell-by date, eg "Your column is still the first
thing we turn to in the magazine each week!",
when your column finished two years ago.

fopulate
noun
A self-conscious and awkward hip wiggle
intended to lure the opposite sex. A move known

39

francy

only by those who learnt to dance towards the
end of the 1980s and in the early 1990s.

francy
noun
Plastic bags you bring back from holiday or a
foreign duty free and use over and over because
you think they look exotic and cool.

fricket
noun
A ball game being played in your local park, by
a large group of expats, whose rules, no matter
how long you observe it, remain a total mystery.

friendevour
noun
A wasted smile, given to someone you believed
was smiling at you, but who was in fact smiling at
the person behind you.

frustrading
noun
Being annoyed with your husband or wife for not
being as annoyed about something as you are.

frynance
noun
What is left of the economy.

funonymity
noun
Phase of adolescence during which it becomes
very important to disguise the fact that you are
having any sort of a good time.

funstable
noun
A policemen who makes a special point of being
chummy and smiley but is secretly just dying
to chain everyone to a radiator and interrogate
them with a big hose.

fupe
abbreviation
Short for 'fagging up the pick ends'.

◆ **fuping**
noun
The process by which a smoker has to ease
himself smoothly back in to the general pub
conversation or with someone being FAGULATED.
See FAGULATION.

furchase

verb

To reflexively say you don't require help from a shop assistant when, in fact, you do, and in two minutes time will approach them for that help.

Gg

gastration

noun

Process of gutting the local boozer and turning it into a gastropub. Remove innards, then scrub and blanch. Poach chef. Tear down walls to reveal kitchen and name pork chops after an English town. Stuff with bare wood, sourdough and fresh, rich clientele. Sprinkle with salty locals for flavour.

gentrance

noun

A toilet door with a sign on it so abstract it is impossible to tell what sex you should to be to enter.

gentrifly

noun

The way posh people like to insert colloquialisms when they are having an argument. "You may hold the view, Barnabus, that your pocket money should be index-linked, but I can tell you right now buster, that ain't gonna happen."

ginstinct

noun

The daunting knowledge that you are about to remember — through hangover fog — something diabolical you did the night before. This pre-recollection phase is vital, enabling you to imagine the worst so reality won't seem so crucifying. However, reality can sometimes not be retrieved, leaving you with severe ALCATHOLICISM.

glotter

noun

Someone who does voiceovers for horror-movie trailers or adverts for luxury puddings. You need a larynx the size of a small church, but the sound can be approximated by reciting "In a world where dogs drive trains," while a friend pours parsley sauce over your face.

⬥ glotting

noun

gobe
noun

A piece of teasing or joke that requires you to nudge the other person with your elbow to make it clear you are just kidding.

godybuard
noun

The ominous, silent dude hovering behind the religious lady who knocks on your door to explain the rules of Hell and give you a leaflet.

gobachov
noun

Oral juggling required to deal with a mouthful of food that is too hot.

goretext
noun

The binding, legally watertight little paragraph that explains how, despite having lost your home and all its contents, you will not be receiving any money from the insurance company.

granuity
noun

Home-prepared meal brought in to work as part

greebie

of an economy drive but devoured by 11am as a pre-lunch snack.

greebie

verb
Trying to look as if you are considering whether or not to buy something you have just had a free taste of at a farmers market, when you know perfectly well you are not going to – possibly because you suspect it to be a case of FARMBANDERY.

grenitch

noun
A person who loves to sniff the back of their watch, and who no longer realises they are doing it in public.

grimtuition

noun
A sixth sense that the person you are with is about to make a horrifically racist or sexist comment, and that you are going to deal with it very badly.

grince

noun
One of the most challenging faces an actor

has to pull, used only at ceremonies when another performer wins an award they were both nominated for. It quickly masks violent disappointment with an air of relief that the judges made, of course, the right decision; the other guy really deserves and needs it.

grinteen
noun
A person at work who is so intense and earnest you have no idea how to arrange your face when you talk to them.

griteful
noun
The demeanour of children who are thanking you for a present because their parents instructed them to say thank you for their presents.

grocernoia
noun
Fear of being judged by the contents of your supermarket trolley — as if anyone cares that you live on Scotch eggs and Jägermeister. Until such time as shops have special 'I'm shopping for my dog' baskets, hide everything under a big bag of baby leaf spinach that you discard at the till.

labravardo

grotuity

noun

An attempt to demonstrate how dissatisfied you are with the food in a restaurant without actually complaining, but by saying "Yes, it was lovely, thank you," in a slightly grumpy way in the hope that your inner thoughts will subliminally connect with the waiter, be reported to the head chef and effect a radical change of cooking policy.

grunday

noun

A day in which it seems impossible to avoid hearing *The Archers* on Radio 4.

gymnauseum

noun

The pool of envious bile that rises when someone you have agreed to meet for a drink arrives shiny and smug because they have managed to do some form of rigorous exercise beforehand, as if you had an unspoken pact to stay unhealthy.

Hh

hadron
noun
An appliance that, despite being slightly faulty, still just about does its job. It annoys you a bit every time you use it, but not enough to actually make you take it back, not least because the malfunction never occurs when anyone else but you is watching.

haemogoblin
noun
A person who gives blood purely for the free tea and biscuits.

halternaters
plural noun
Pedestrians who really enjoy officiously stopping

the traffic on behalf of people trying to reverse their cars into parking spaces.

handelabra
noun
Awkward moment of fumbling that is the result of two incompatible handshakes meeting, such as when a person offers a high-five, some jazz-related tomfoolery or shoulder bumping in response to your traditional outstretched mitt. The remedy is to disable their ghetto antics by bear-hugging them like a long-lost friend.

hangler
noun
The guy at a party that no one seems to know. An expert in hangling will start at a big function, then attach him/herself to a smaller subsection of friends, including yourself, that decides to leave. This whittling process continues until there are just two of you and you are naked.

hawkyprop
noun
A person who walks with a cane, not because they need it, but because they think it looks cool.

hedge'n'wedge

noun

A kind of trustafarian hairdo that is daubed with product and painstakingly arranged in front of the bathroom mirror to look scruffy or absent-minded. This roughly translates as: "I just woke up on my mezzanine under a 12-string guitar. I dreamt I had no moolah. Intense."

♦ **hedge'n'wedger**

noun

hellbellies

noun

Annoying English family you just can't shake on holiday. They get on the same flight, check in at the same hotel and eat in the same 'secret' restaurant only the locals know about. Even if you go and hide inside an active volcano they will find you and tell you they come here every year.

hellocopters

plural noun

People who use your name too frequently in the first few minutes of meeting you in order to make themselves remember it for the future, the problem being that it makes them quite

annoying, so you have made a mental note not to
see them ever again.

historectomy
noun
A procedure used in film and TV productions
whereby all the annoying historical accuracy is
removed from a costume drama in order to make
way for more heaving boobs.

hobbut
noun
The one switch on a holiday hire-car whose
function is an intriguing but total mystery, and
that you are slightly afraid to activate.

hoebylo
noun
The telephone call you make purely in order to
say goodbye to someone, having been cut off by
the mobile network just before saying it at the
end of the previous conversation. You then get
their voicemail, requiring the other party to call
you back to say hello and confirm receipt of the
goodbye.

hoittle
plural noun
Aggressive yet careful manoeuvres required to
initiate the flow of tomato ketchup from a newly
opened bottle.

horrigami
noun
A wretched point reached in the folding
of a map, the packing away of a tent, or the
untangling of a kite where it seems conceivable
that you will be trying to accomplish this one
task for the rest of your life.

hundread
noun
Doomed panic caused by overexposure to
supplements telling you of 100 things you must
do, see or eat before you die.

hypoteasis
noun
The scientific impossibility of the second cup of
tea in the morning tasting as good as the first.

Ii

ignostic

noun

The feeling when a friend doesn't notice that you make what feels like quite substantial alterations to your appearance or lifestyle, such as getting hair extensions, suddenly wearing top hats or having a sex change.

illubriation

noun

The (completely fallacious) realisation that you are able to explain very complex things when you are drunk.

indignatries

plural noun

People who relish taking offence — and who never feel more joyously alive than when they

infirmation

are absolutely livid. Keen not to miss out on any chance to wield the pitchfork of disgruntlement, indignatries can even back-date their disgust to cover events they missed or that in no way bothered them at the time.

infirmation

noun

The descent into panic that is inevitably produced by self-diagnosis on the internet — a series of Google searches that builds from the gentle enquiry of 'Why does my chin feel warm?' to the panic of 'Strange flesh-eating viruses', 'How long have I got?' and 'Tips on painless euthanasia'.

inflatulation

noun

Branch of marketing that puts the description of mundane objects and professions on steroids until they sound like dialogue from a secret agent movie. 'Vitamin pill' becomes 'nutrient delivery system', 'bag' becomes 'strap-enabled item relocation engine' and someone who makes up words becomes a 'contemporary lexicon-introduction engineer'.

interwoo
noun
The art of pretending to understand what small children are talking about. It is embarrassing to keep using the parents as interpreters, but admitting to them you have no idea what their frothing nappysack is on about always feels uncomfortably close to saying they have given birth to a loser.

ipswitch
noun
The track your iPod always seems to want to play when you turn it on, however randomly you order it to behave. Quite possibly something by Leo Sayer.

irituality
noun
Unique form of annoyed disappointment caused by finding *Songs of Praise* on the TV.

ironside
noun
The solidly-held belief that you could represent yourselves in an American court of law as a result of all the movies you have seen.

Jj

jargonaut
noun
An unwieldy sentence composed entirely of
incomprehensible bureaucratic lingo.

jaundry
noun
The colour of tired, overwashed clothes.
Eventually they will become CRUSTICS.

jazzturbation
noun
Vocalist trait of manipulating an imaginary
instrument in mid-air to represent the flow of
notes during a scat solo — a kind of musical
sign-language for the hard of hearing.
◊ jazzturbator

jetblag

noun

A brainy, aspirational magazine that you only ever buy in an airport bookshop. You have always fancied reading it and this flight offers an excellent opportunity to catch up on the latest gossip in quantum philosophy circles. At 30,000ft, the extent of your delusion becomes clear and you borrow a copy of *Hello*.

nibstery

Kk

karatea
plural noun
Exotic infusions from the makers of more traditional English brews, packaged with oriental mystery suggestive of inner peace, cleansing and the taste of wee.

klimpy
noun
Satisfying feeling of having paid for a coffee by offloading the huge amount of loose change in your pocket, which turned out to amount to exactly the right figure. Often scuppered by the discovery, as you count out the final coin, that it is a TVINK.

Ll

labravardo
noun

Confident air you adopt when an enormous,
unleashed dog is bounding towards you in a
park. You do this because you read somewhere
that dogs can smell fear, and this is an attempt
to mask that odour. As the dog escapes with your
liver, be reassured that he is 'only playing'.

laptopia
plural noun

Cute stickers, cases and folksy adornments
people decorate their laptops with in order to
give them a human touch – and to stave off the
rising fear of machines developing consciousness
and laying waste to mankind.

lecreusing

noun

1. Lustful wandering in kitchenware departments trying to convince yourself that an £80 slatted spoon is an important addition to your culinary tools.

2. The belief men hold that they are safe perving at girls in said department since they will assume you are in some way enlightened.

lentl

noun

An attempt at giving up drinking that fails before 8pm the same day.

lexcrete

verb

To produce a book of made-up words.

♦ **lexcretion**

noun

The act of producing a book of made-up words.

libobia

noun

Fear of running out of things to read on holiday, resulting in the purchase of large quantities of JETBLAG at the airport.

librido
noun
Specific form of sublimated sexual tension found only in libraries.

lingrid
noun
The odd, rather joyless person you only tangentially know who is the first — and unsettlingly early — arrival at your house party.

littoris
noun
A person who takes a statement of fact and tries to make it even more definite by adding the word 'literally', eg "He literally just walked in through that door there, the one that literally allows people in and out of the building."

lostinato
verb
To repeatedly look in the same cupboard or drawer something should be in, even though it isn't.
♦ **lostinator**
noun
One who *lostinatos*.

lostrich

noun

A person who, having stopped you to ask for directions, listens very carefully to your comprehensive and detailed information and proceeds in completely the wrong direction. Can be a result of MAPATHY.

lutter

noun

The mess of a betting shop or racecourse after an important meet.

Mm

mapathy

noun

The dispiriting knowledge, even as you ask someone for directions, that your brain is not going to take in any information beyond the first instruction, "Take the first left …" You will then need to immediately ask another local for directions, thereby giving the first person you approached a complex about coming across as somewhat unstable or untrustworthy.

masochiato

noun

A rich and indulgent hot drink that has had all of its rich and indulgent ingredients removed.

mathemagician
noun

A market stall owner or minicab driver who
pretends to be working out what your groceries
or your journey is going to cost, but is clearly just
going to invent a figure in a few seconds time.

mazerrat
noun

A driver who flashes their lights and honks their
horn at every turn in the road, so they can drive
at 110mph but still appear to be concerned with
road safety.

mebarrassment
noun

Carbon offsetting, but for the ego — a way
of having a good old boast about something
and then neutralising it with self-deprecation
eg "God, I've just been at a dinner party with
Robert De Niro. All these amazing people and
then me, a nobody. So embarassing!".

mecycling
verb

To add a comment to your own blog, after five
desperate minutes of BLOGORRHOEA.

melady
noun
A track on your CD player that you have to keep repeating because you want it to be on when your new date arrives and he/she is late.

menapplause
noun
A period of uncertainty, after some kind of presentation, as to whether it is appropriate to clap, and as to who will be the first to put their hands together. In music, this welcome hiatus is often spoilt by CLAPPERAZZI.

mewth
noun
The taste of having slept very soon after lunch.

minisery
noun
The deflation that used to be caused by turning on the television and discovering that the programme you are excited to have found being broadcast is either a) just about to finish or b) 'to be continued'.

minstrole

noun

A person who believes, for reasons difficult to fathom, that it is perfectly reasonable and thrifty to return a half-eaten chocolate to an assortment box.

misfartune

noun

Despite not having seen a soul for hours, the sudden arrival of a totally beautiful stranger at precisely the moment you consider it safe to break wind.

mobble

noun

The way people who are old enough to remember the first telephone number of the village operate mobile phones. The device is held, in two hands, as if it were an antique teacup, and there is a tangible sense of triumph after any pressing of a button that doesn't lead directly to a baffling technical disaster.

mogleby

noun

The one guy at a stag party who looks

moog

desperately uncomfortable slotting money down a woman's G-string.

moog

noun
The mouth of a soloing jazz guitarist in full flow.

motorbloat

noun
The anaesthetized, 'You don't exist' stare passengers in luxury 4x4s give pedestrians — the result of travelling in the vehicular equivalent of an intensive care unit.

mowplin

noun
A sense that cutting the grass should have given you a greater feeling of satisfaction than it has.

mugoo

noun
A face – designed to express neutrality, innocence and honesty – that you put on especially for the police.

mulder
noun
A creeping desire in old people to ignore — and be enraged by — sell-by dates.

multimediocre
noun
Just about everything.

twango

Nn

nadaday
noun

What appears to be a really dynamic working day — full of progress and post-its and high-fives. But mysteriously, despite this blizzard of productivity, when you add it up, the net result is that you have achieved absolutely nothing. Had you stayed in the toilet all day, your life would have advanced further.

◆ **nadadayer**
noun

nadvent
noun

Sense of deflation caused by a return to everyday life after an episode of déjà vu that you have tried very hard to REMEMULATE.

nazimuth

noun

Someone who insists on bringing up Hitler during an argument about how popular something is, reminding you that, "Yes, well, Hitler was a very popular politician, don't forget."

neeyairs

noun

The deliberately opaque response you have to give to a query from a boring person or HANGLER when you realise you weren't really listening and have no idea what question you are answering and whether 'yes' or 'no' is the right avenue to pick.

nerrwinnies

plural noun

People who believe that, when faced with a point in an argument that completely exposes their position and drowns them in a vat of their own wrongness, they can somehow still come out victorious if they just repeat the winning idea back to their opponent in a silly voice.

newpid

noun

A piece of expensive, untouched technology

that makes you feel slightly sick when you find it gathering dust in a drawer, because you purchased it purely to be in possession of the latest gadget. It has never been used and is now obsolete.

nibstery

noun

Being convinced, by some sensory mischief between your mouth and brain, that you still have one more bite left of the snack you have just been enjoying; except you can't find it. According to the evidence, you have either eaten it, or the morsel has slipped through a wormhole in the continuity of space, to take its place in a high-calorie parallel universe composed entirely of treats.

nimyum

noun

The sound of a congregation that doesn't quite know the tune of a hymn, or that of many people UMBLIBLING.

nopples

plural noun

Plastic ring-pulls on milk cartons that are

nostalgebra

designed to break just before they have fulfilled their task.

nostalgebra

noun
Branch of mathematics used to predict exactly when any group of thirty-somethings will start to reminisce about sweets and toys such as Spangles and Stretch Armstrong. Also handy for calculating how big Mars bars really used to be, and how many viewings of *I Love the 1980s* a human being can withstand.

nostroll

noun
A walk taken — suddenly and purposefully — purely to avoid the results of one's own flatulence and implicate others in its creation.

novada

noun
Brief, exciting state of mind during which it seems as if you understand the workings of the US presidential election. You rush to find a water cooler at which to practice sounding casual about New Hampshire, Super Tuesday and article two of the US constitution, but suddenly it's all gone. What is 'federal' again?

novulating

verb

Obsessively clicking on to Amazon to see how well your book is doing in the sales ranking.

nulties

plural noun

Middle-class people who think it is cool to GENTRIFLY the UK police as 'Five-O', 'Narcs' or 'Feds', as if they have recently become a drug hopper in Baltimore rather than a purchaser of aged parmesan.

Oo

oadlingers
plural noun
People in small villages who derive a rich sense of fulfilment from informing visitors they are driving the wrong way down a one-way street.

oozone
noun
Facial expression of comfort used by actors in commercials for hot drinks, soothing lozenges or phallic ice creams.

optickle
noun
A strong, unexpected urge to giggle when an optician gets very close to your face and says "Does it look better like this? Or like this? Like this? Or this?".

orcastration
noun
Impotent rage felt after being put on hold for
20 minutes accompanied by a short repeating
section of Vivaldi's *Four Seasons.*

orchasm
noun
The horrifying gulf between the picture of
compatibility your imagination conjures up
as you prepare for a blind date and what gets
served up by the cold hand of reality. They too
would find lapdancing for their grandparents
less embarrassing.

organidler
noun
Someone who suddenly finds mundane chores
alluring in the face of important work; a
seductive belief, for instance, that the genius of
your long-awaited collection of haikus will flow
more bounteously after a quick sock amnesty.
Organidling is like a career condom, allowing you
to feel productive without producing any results.

overwoden
noun
A place you are trying to get to on holiday that

overwoden

you keep being told is just around the next
corner or beyond the next hill — but is, in fact,
a small town on wheels that the tourist-shy
inhabitants can drive away to prevent curious
travellers ever reaching it.

Pp

paldroth
noun
Tea, as produced by vending machines.

panicdote
noun
A hastily improvised story to explain why you are wearing your wife's wedding dress.

panterbury
noun
A CLOAD made entirely of trousers.

panticlimax
noun
The realisation, as you get undressed, that the

pantom

person you are about to sleep with is wearing
PUNDERWEAR.

pantom
noun
Anything you do in the toilet that doesn't seem
to be there when you get up to flush.

pedestriumph
noun
The look of righteous supremacy you direct at
the driver of a car you forced to stop at a zebra
crossing.

pedify
noun
An attempt to remember, when trying new shoes
on in a shop, how you normally walk.
◆ **pedifying**
adjective

pennis
noun
The game, favoured by a certain kind of blazer-
by-the-fireside gent, of playing with the loose
change in their pocket, tantalisingly close to their
balls.

pfoffter

noun

A kind of hollow laugh that flops out of the mouth lethargically and is delivered without a smile, used to acknowledge that in some situations or frames of mind what the other person just said could be amusing to some people, but that it doesn't really work for you. Try it now.

philantropy

noun

Trapped sense of deflation upon realising that the conversation you have let yourself get drawn into is the beginning of an extended and complex story that will climax in you being asked for some change.

philosoppy

noun

The inverse correlation between the epic complexity of scientific theories (the origins of the universe, the duality of light, quantum mechanics and relativity) and the names they end up with (big bang, Schrödinger's cat, string).

wiggot

phonelation
noun
Intense — and slightly shameful — sense of light-headed relief experienced when a call you are dreading is met by an answerphone, thereby allowing you to deliver very uncomfortable news and run away.

pieromaniac
noun
A person who has an overwhelming desire to burn down classic examples of Grade II listed seaside architecture.
◆ **pieromania**
noun

pilger
verb
To locate something in a safe place that you will then forget.

pillickle
noun
The practice of anally labelling your food in the fridge in an attempt to prevent GREABING.

pitroll
noun
An in-car picnic.

plusfourbia
noun
Fear of golf in all its forms, 'crazy' or otherwise.

plutter
noun
The cringey, manufactured laugh you have to psyche yourself up for when you realise you've already heard the complicated anecdote or joke your friend is telling. Unfortunately, they are past the point at which you could stop them without seeming rude. A form of platonic fake orgasm.

polterguest
noun
The person who kips over at your house after a late night and goes in the morning without saying goodbye or leaving a note.

poosham
plural noun
Absurd scientific ingredients that cosmetics adverts say are an essential part of haircare products — but may well just be margarine or

an old line from a *Buck Rogers* script. "Now with added NitroPenty Waxyloin47, which interviews every individual strand of hair and forces any without supermodel ambition to fall out!".

posanthropist
noun
One of those unnerving people who becomes increasingly chipper and can-do the more things go disastrously wrong, guffawing away at the end of every sentence, even if that sentence is: "Oh my God, my life is in tatters." As the Titanic sank, they would have asked the violinist for a quick lesson.

pototoes
plural noun
Cute malapropisms and slips of the tongue young children make. This whole thing is a scam to distract you from what they have just left in your shoe. Babies are born with a perfect vocabulary, but are careful not to use it until they have got the hang of a toilet.

poutburst
noun
Special face people unconsciously pull in front of the mirror in a clothes shop. A futile

pramble

attempt to see what you look like when you're
not looking at yourself, or a panic to bridge the
gap between your self-image and the shambling
person you see before you.

pramble

noun
Process by which one tries to learn
surreptitiously the rules of an unfamiliar
institution (first-class airport lounge, courthouse,
sex shop), while simultaneously trying to appear
as if one has been coming for a decade. Despite
seeming to be perfectly at home, PRAMBLERS never
know where the toilets are.

prawk

noun
A canapé of uncertain provenance.

prawl

noun
The pose you will find someone in if you turn
the light on in a room they are trying to cross in
the dark.

predictaball

noun
The way that playing some variation of squash in

a a dark room, wearing luminescent pants, was how science fiction movies from the end of the 20th century depicted the sport of the future.

priminals
plural noun
Old ladies who compulsively steal napkins, individually packaged portions of butter and sugar from museum cafés.

psalmon
noun
A fish that has been blessed.

punalysis
noun
A prickly feeling of panic induced by getting stuck in the middle of a complicated joke. You may have inadvertently spilled the punch line early, forgotten what the bishop was doing on top of the actress in the first place, or realised that the gag is totally offensive to that guy in the wheelchair.

punderwear
noun
Any pant or item of lingerie that has a joke on it – and, when worn, a joke in it.

Qq

quackrobats

noun

Someone who is always trying a new form of
bizarre alternative therapy for a complicated
ailment they quite clearly haven't even got.

quanecdote

noun

A special kind of question — asked by an
audience member at a Q&A with, say, a famous
film director — designed purely to show off how
much the questioner already knows, and allow
them to tell a meandering, irrelevant story about
themselves.

queasing

noun

Anxious, clenched-teeth smile people put on – as

if a balloon was about to burst in their face –
when they need to ask a very awkward question
or favour.

quebble
verb
To claim that you are not annoyed by something
even though it is abundantly clear you are.
Quebblers, it should be noted, have often been
dragooned in to being annoyed by an AGROBAT.
♦ **quebbler**
noun

queuthanasia
noun
The sapping of energy caused by lining up
behind someone at a busy cash machine, railway-
ticket dispenser or supermarket till who, despite
having minutes of idle preparation time, only
begins the five-minute fumble for their bankcard
when the machine bleeps to request payment.
Delay makes machine cancel; and the whole
process repeats.

qunt
noun
A person who, as a last resort or sine qua non,
drops in a bit of Latin during an argument in

an effort to intimidate an opponent they see as poorly schooled — but is clearly outwitting them at every turn.

Rr

refleshment

noun

The reserve spurt of energy joggers deploy, even though they are so exhausted they could throw up their own heart, when passing someone who looks sexy. Body language is quickly transformed from flailing sweatbox to: "I'm fit — and so are you baby. Let's work out." Once safely out of sight, they fall over.

rememulate

noun

A futile attempt – having realised you are experiencing an episode of déjà vu – to make it last as long as possible.

rememulate

noun

A futile attempt – having realised you are experiencing an episode of déjà vu – to make it last as long as possible.

reyonion

noun

Having bumped in to someone you haven't seen for years and caught up, the awkwardness of what to do when you bump in to them again just two hours later.

ritzing

noun

Uncontrollable cleptomania brought on by bedrooms in hotels. The urge is usually triggered by the sight of miniature bottles of posh shower gel; then it's pens, slippers, notepads, bath robes and flannels. The only thing not worth taking is the ridiculous kettle, which was designed to be used by mice.

romanstipation

noun

Not yet feeling comfortable enough to break wind in the presence of a lover.

roundabort

noun

Tortuous Artful Dodger pocket-fumbling,
intended to show great willingness at the bar —
but which is clearly not going to reveal a wallet
anytime soon. Like the Wild West played in
reverse, the aim is to be the last to draw.

wimblows

Ss

sardones
plural noun
Wordless noises of suspicion or disbelief
produced by presenters of the *Today* programme
during interviews.

sconeoisseur
noun
A singular member of the local church parish
who believes you can tell all you need to know
about people through the quality of their home
baking, and who will always rate those talents
('sconeupmanship') higher than, for instance,
anything annoyingly Christian such as putting an
end to world hunger.

screbe
noun
The sound of an orchestra tuning up.

seeoseekay
noun
Parental trick of communicating words such as 'cock' when there are children in the room who should be in 'B', 'E', 'D'.

self-efaecing
noun
The hope of gaining integrity points by voicing a criticism you have of yourself, spoilt by then getting annoyed that people agree with your self-assessment.

selfilmportance
noun
The forbiddingly cool atmosphere created by movie crews — through the use of big lights, rain machines and hazard tape — that makes you feel like a pest for needing to get through your front door while they are filming in your street. Actually, they are deeply envious you can do that, rather than having to babysit a smoke machine until 4am.

shniftcuck

noun

What comes out of your mouth when you are forced to abandon a really high-quality piece of swearing mid-flow — normally because a child, granny or archbishop has wandered in to the room. Leaves a nagging feeling of unfinished business, like u-turning on a pee or a sneeze.

shoppingpong

noun

A form of vicarious consumerism whereby, having browsed happily in a DVD shop and amassed a huge pile of discounted, must-see films, you gradually put them all back, queasy at your retail gluttony, and leave.

shrinkling

noun

An attempt to make the opening of a packet of crisps or sweets in a quiet place less disturbing by doing it very gradually. The result magnifies the unease for all concerned while prolonging the episode — like trying to shout really gently and slowly.

slyrillic

noun

The way middle-aged men show they are still youthful by reciting pop lyrics (eg "Bet you wish your girlfriend was hot like me") but in an ironic tone of voice to make it clear they are beyond all that stuff.

sloup

noun

Stock that sits there on the stove for a week after the Sunday roast, and is endlessly reheated and fed with leftovers until it becomes a Frankenstein's monster of a meal.

smearcats

plural noun

Posh, pretentious graffiti artists that go to work in parts of town that were previously 'edgy' but are now swarming with hipster geeks. A big cartoon cock and balls, or a spot of tagging, will no longer do, and walls fill up with philosophies such as "Solid configuration of chance events".

smellières

noun

An instinctive feeling that you should have

used the word 'lavatory' instead of 'toilet' in a Michelin-starred restaurant.

smirl
noun
A reluctant kind of facial greeting that uses all the same muscles as a smile but keeps the mouth straight and lifts the eyebrows a little. *Smirling* at someone is a friendly acknowledgement of them that nonetheless makes it clear you can't be arsed to talk to them.

smorkler
noun
A lone person in the theatre or cinema who brings in lots of food, and who, despite the heart-tearing display of man's inhumanity to man being dramatised on the stage or screen, mysteriously finds the whole production hilarious.

smugshot
noun
Relief at seeing a childhood picture of an especially good-looking person and realising that at one stage in their life they did at least have the decency to look gormless.

smumf
noun
The oblivious snuffling and heavy breathing of someone who has headphones on.
♦ **smumfer**
noun
One who smumfs.

smuttering
noun
Especially pompous and high-minded tone used to shame pornography and its viewers by people who secretly have a stash of jazz mags at home.

snewz
noun
The early phase of an all-night election broadcast —when information is hard to come by and presenters are forced to reheat the same old soup of facts while playing tag: "Back to you, Nigel", "Thanks Gemma. Francis, how are things looking on the ground?", "Well Nigel, voters are definitely walking with their feet." etc.

snoobing
verb
Pretending to be asleep during a train journey

because you are bored of talking to the person next to you.

sobjectivity
noun
The return of calm, rational thoughts after a good blub – or in the case of children, after getting what they want.

socceratease
plural noun
Men at weddings who are really nervy about meeting new people until the conversation turns to football, at which point they confidently philosophise about love, life and the beautiful game.

sodcast
noun
Music, on a crowded bus, coming from the speaker on a mobile phone. *Sodcasters* are terrified of not being noticed, so they spray their audio wee around the place like tomcats.

soldy
noun
The pleasing smell of new audio, video or computer equipment.

spannock
noun
An entirely useless free 'tool' that arrives with flatpack furniture.

spantonese
noun
The language of the DIY shop. You carefully learn the exact name of the part you need (instead of just a 'bendy bit') but as with most foreign tongues get scuppered by a follow-up query: "Do you want that for a flapping tri-nipple? Or the old-fashioned coil-and-soil gasket?"

spune
noun
Involuntary, melodically pointless humming used in situations where silence is uncomfortable but talking is also inappropriate, such as pub toilets. *Spuning* can also indicate barely-containable rage that you are trying to damp down.
◆ **spuner**
noun

sputnak
noun
A shy morsel of food that emerges from a corner of your mouth some hours after a meal.

spweek
noun
The voice you need to present TV for very young children.

squarrel
noun
An argument you psyche yourself up for, only to find the person you were expecting to combat agrees with everything you say – leaving a restless surfeit of mental energy.

squift
noun
An inability to continue a conversation upon entering a lift.

statustician
noun
Someone whose job seems to consist entirely of explaining to people how busy and important they are.

stockports

noun

A fear of interacting with vending machines.

suckwit

noun

The attempt to not sound out of breath during a conversation with someone you fancy, having bumped into them at the gym.

swarping

noun

Dispiriting ritual that spectacle wearers are forced through whereby people insist on trying on your glasses, and seem bemused at your reluctance to let them play with something you rely on totally to get through every day of your life. Your reward, once they get them off you, will be: "My God, your eyes are fucked!" Like borrowing someone's prosthetic leg and saying: "Wow, you must be really crap at walking!".

sweeny

noun

Ominous evidence that your new hairdresser, behind their decoy smile, is more nervous than you are.

Tt

tangoat

noun

The particularly sexy person who, to your surprise and delight, suddenly appears to show a great deal of interest in your solitary dance moves, but who spends the whole time sneaking a look over your shoulder at their date, who they are punishing for being flirty with an ex.

tannoyance

noun

Endless, semi-coherent burbling on trains about beverages, station stops and "your personal own private possessions and items and luggage and bags and individual property before you leave the station at the next stop" delivered with ear-bleeding feedback or through speakers that make everything sound like a bee in a jar.

yakpacker

teunuchs
plural noun
People who spend much of their time
TUNICLYCLING, and who like to pause when their
phone rings to let you hear the full aggravating
symphony before they answer.

texacto
noun
The obsessive compulsion to make sure your
final bill on a petrol pump is an exact number of
pounds and no pence.

thespadrills
plural noun
Performers who insist on demonstrating, even if
they are just in a supermarket queue, that they have
been trained in an obscure French conservatoire to
use their bodies in an advanced and expressive way
that requires an awful lot of stretching.

titlerate
noun
Feeling compelled to say aloud and snigger at any
unusual names from the credits at the end of a movie.
♦ **titlerater**
noun

tolkeen
verb
To find yourself compelled to hunt for books you already own when browsing in a bookshop.

toylet
plural noun
Fun objects, cartoon seats and wipes made to convince children that using the lavatory the grown-up way can really be as much fun as just filling your pants.

transflemation
noun
That empathetic, itchy feeling you get at the back of your mouth when talking to someone who really needs to clear their throat — your body working out a way of coughing on behalf of someone who can't be bothered.

transister
noun
Someone who used to be your brother.

transmushion
noun
Sloth-like approach to reality caused by watching too many episodes of a TV show in

one sitting. If you still hear lead characters arguing when the DVD is switched off, then fantasy levels are running so high that your own life is going to seem as exciting as a cardboard toilet.

trapporia
noun
A restaurant with a colossal menu of dishes all covered in the same sauce.

travis
noun
The gulf between how good you claim your time was at a music festival and how good it really was.

treasurance
plural noun
The hours you have spent in your life discussing and working out what you would do with a million pound win on the lottery.

treatease
noun
The inability to resist revealing to someone in advance that you have found the perfect birthday present for them (even, in some cases, when no

trumptin

thought has actually been given to the matter).
This constitutes an 'emotional advance', a way of
getting on credit some of the eventual happiness
of the recipient.

trumptin
noun
A container or box that a purchase was packaged
in, which you feel is slightly too good to just
throw away, despite having no idea what else you
could put in it.

tunicycling
noun
The grating sound of someone sifting through
the various ringtones on their cellphone in an
effort to find the one, suicidally naff loop that
best projects the remains of their personality.
See also TEUNUCHS.

tvink
noun
A foreign coin that seems to be following
you.

twango
noun

A little dance your nervous system does when it has clearly got the wrong end of the stick, eg picking up an empty kettle you thought was full, climbing a step that turns out not to be there, or the taste of coffee when your mouth is expecting tea.

twatnav
noun

A person whose concept of taking charge of the mapreading while you drive consists of them going quiet for long stretches of road and occasionally issuing retrospective instructions such as: "We should have done a left back there."

twatter
verb

To broadcast your life — via a series of mundane online updates — instead of living it.

twotney
noun

Anyone who has memorised all the two-letter words in order to be better at Scrabble®.

tyrantulas

plural noun

The various pets kept by Bond villains and other evil geniuses.

Uu

umbibling

noun

The sound you make if you are reluctant or embarrassed to say the Lord's Prayer out loud.

unstabulary

noun

Feeling a frisson of ghoulish excitement because it looks as if you are about to witness a police drama kick off in the street, only to have the thrill deflated by realising that it's a bunch of Police Community Support Officers in pursuit of a piece of litter.

unsurient

noun

Wanting something to eat, but having no idea what.

Vv

vaguerant

noun

Someone who makes a solid arrangement to come and visit you next week, but who becomes increasingly hard to pin down as the day of the appointment draws closer until, at the chosen hour, they call to see if you fancy coming to see them instead.

vanisette

plural noun

Spectacularly pretty people who always claim to be looking 'really, really rough' today.

vidiots

plural noun

A group of people at a dinner party struggling to

return to regular conversation after watching too many YouTube clips.

voib
noun

A Yiddish word or expression that you really enjoy using, despite a nagging sense you have no idea what it actually means.

Ww

wablet

noun

Frantic, camp little wave you give to help someone spot you in a situation – such as an auction – where you don't want to draw any attention to yourself.

waftersun

noun

The little pocket of holiday air that travels back home with you, sealed inside a suitcase. As you unpack, for a precious second you are back there — beachside hotel, pianist tinkling away, squinting at the sunset through the lens of a perfect martini, surrounded by dirty underwear.

waitrogues

plural noun

Cars that glide malevolently around supermarket car parks, like sharks in a tank, waiting to see if you are about to vacate a parking spot.

weavesdropping

noun

Annoying way that people who insist they can continue a hobby – for example knitting – while watching a TV programme keep needing to ask you for an update on the plot.

welthamstow

noun

The demeaning audition you have to go through after hailing a London taxi in the small hours, as if your address represents some sort of proposal of marriage. The final oh-go-on-then shrug is to remind you that money is not sufficient: you must have the gratitude of the nude winter hitchhiker.

wenking

verb

To swiftly pretend to have something in your eye in order to disguise what you now realise was

yinching

a totally inappropriate wink at someone else's girlfriend.

noun

A very posh form of masturbation.

werty

plural noun

Futuristic and ergonomic 'improvements' on the standard computer keyboard that never catch on.

wessle

verb

To massage the pipe and shake the nozzle of a petrol pump to get the most for your money. See also TEXACTO.

westrogen

noun

The hormone that makes men want to form boy bands.

whasper

noun

Half-voice used to communicate with someone who can't hear you through a shop window. The need to make clear, lip-readable gestures is very difficult without actually talking. But if you talk it

wittingstall

looks as if you're sharing somewhat too publicly your intention of nipping to the chemist.

wittingstall

noun

The art of pretending to have missed what someone said in order to buy yourself a little extra time to consider your response.

wiggot

noun

The random object you are forced to stare at, with real intention and curiosity, which lies just above and to the left of the person whose eyes you meet after you turn round too soon after your friend says: "Don't look now, but there's a really freaky looking guy behind you."

wikognize

noun

The ability, on the phone, to sound as if the answer to a question is painfully obvious — when in fact what you have done is quickly look it up on the internet, put it in your own words and effect a casual 'just browsing round my brain' tone of voice.

willipede

noun

An insurance micturation done not because one is needed, but because it will be quite a while before the next toilet stop.

willpapering

noun

Decorating a room in your house in tiny patches over a period of months. A kind of attention deficit DIY.

wimblows

plural noun

The two old ladies who, upon entering a huge cinema in which you are the only viewer, decide to sit right next to you and bypass the film in favour of a good catch-up.

winceybago

noun

The odd walk you do when passing through an airport metal detector. You try to appear all casual and non-explosive, but clench up as the moment of scanning approaches, giving rise to an odd, robotic gait.

winjury
noun
Sprain or muscle damage caused by trying to get fit by playing a Nintendo®.

witherspoon
noun
A delightful evening whose atmosphere is soured by an increasingly futile and aggravated search for somewhere still open to have one last drink.

witrat
noun
The annoyance felt at yourself for pretending to have read a novel, because the person you are trying to impress now seems to want a conversation about its literary merits. See also BIOGRAFEAR.

woobris
plural noun
Overconfident trees.

wotang
noun
Unexpected burst of rapping from someone who really has no business getting up on the microphone and spitting it (see Debbie Harry,

John Barnes, Dee Dee Ramone, George Michael, any priests). Like cellists 'rocking out', the results are as comfortable as purchasing pornography from your parents.

wrencheslas
noun
A beautifully machined and very specialised-looking object whose quality makes it difficult to throw away. It has lived in your toolbox for 20 years, during which you have never found a use for it. It will be there when you die. Ideally a wrencheslas should be stored in a TRUMPTIN.

Yy

yahsbos
noun
A form of punishment, normally having to take tea with poor people, for misbehaving YOBES.

yakpackers
plural noun
People who aimlessly plod about when speaking on their mobiles. Some amble round in slow-motion circles, getting in the way of pedestrians, others absent-mindedly kick the kerb as if trying to wake a sleeping dog. Especially distracting is the wittering zombie who marches up and down in front of your window seat in a restaurant.
♦ **yakpacking**
noun

yenoney
noun

A person who has lost sight of the difference between 'yes' and 'no', and just uses the words interchangeably. They say things like, "Yeah, no, totally" and "No, I completely agree, yeah." They are useless in court cases, marriages — and on automated telephone booking lines for cinemas.

yessop
noun

Person sitting next to you in the theatre, cinema or lecture room who looks around to make sure everyone has noticed how alive they are to the subtle nuances of the show. Will often be accompanied by their more vocal equivalent, the FANCHOVY.

yesticle
noun

The special friend who you don't really like that much, but who is useful to wheel out now and again because they agree and sympathise with everything you say, and can somehow find nuggets of optimistic gold in all the parts of your life that have turned to shit.

yesticulation

noun

Demented grinning and nodding radio
interviewers have to do in order to communicate
"Yes! Excellent! Please say more!" to their
interviewee without actually saying it. See also
YESTICLE.

yinching

noun

Sympathetic facial gymnastics and tongue
squirming that you can't help doing when a
friend tells you of how they were recently stung
in the mouth by a bee, or had eight hours of root
canal from a partially competent dentist.

yoast

noun

Embarrassing and aggressive marketing attempts
to make breakfast cereals and healthy foods
appeal to teenagers.

yobes

plural noun

Posh kids who pretend they grew up on mean
streets. Yobes will often GENTRIFLY and grow up to
become NULTIES.

yolter
verb
To address someone in a very loud voice at precisely the moment a room goes very quiet.

yoybles
plural noun
The colourful, undulating patterns that swirl behind your lids when you rub your eyes forcefully. This is your brain's screensaver.

yuleogy
noun
The excruciating, cooing appreciation you have to show for a Christmas present you would rather throw on the fire. Despite your bluff about having admired these in the shops or thought one of them could be really useful in the kitchen, you are horrified by this misinterpretation of your personality.

Zz

zentropy

noun

The feeling of talking to people on drugs when you are not.

zinquix

noun

A combination of letters that you wish to God meant something during a game of Scrabble®.